I0762358

GRANDPA,
I made you a
BOOK

DEAR GRANDPA,

I made this book for you because you're an amazing grandpa.

Thank you for all that you do and all the ways you help me grow. I've included some of them here in these pages, but there are just too many to fit into one book.

I made this especially for you because you really are one of a kind.

Love,

HERE'S ME!

You and I are SPECIAL to each other.

You know I like...

And I know you like...

WE LOVE EACH OTHER SO MUCH! HERE, I DREW A PICTURE OF US TOGETHER:

You are
one of my
favorite
people
because...

I wonder what you were like when you were my age.

You must have been

even back then!

One thing that always reminds me of you is ______________________ ______________________.

Here's a picture of it
to remind you of me!

I love spending time with you.

I especially like when we ________

________.

I'm so proud that you're my grandpa. I'll even announce it on this plane:

I have so many fun memories with you!

Here's a picture of us when we ______ ______ so we can always remember.

If I could give you some of your favorite things, I'd give you...

You are one of the coolest people I know. You might be cooler than...

(check the boxes)

- [ ] Finding a dinosaur bone

ADMIT ONE

- [ ] Front row Seats to a Sports game

- [ ]

(WRITE YOUR OWN!)

So, here's a
BIG THANK-YOU
HIGH FIVE
for being so awesome.

(Trace hand)

You deserve a GAZILLION MORE!

You really are important to me. When I grow up, I hope I'm as

____

as you are.

HERE,
LET ME
GIVE YOU
THIS
AWARD.

WORLD'S
GRANDPA

Thank you, Grandpa.
Because of you, I know that...

(check the boxes)

☐ You are always there for me

☐ We'll have lots more ADVENTURES

☐

(WRITE YOUR OWN!)

BECAUSE
OF YOU,
WE ARE A
FAMILY.

Written by: Miriam Hathaway
Illustrated by: Asahi Nagata
Edited by: Bailey Vega
Art Directed by: Justine Edge

An imprint of the Crown Publishing Group
A division of Penguin Random House LLC
1745 Broadway, New York, NY 10019
live-inspired.com | penguinrandomhouse.com

ISBN: 978-1-957891-71-2 | CPSIA: A012509001

1st printing. Manufactured in China with soy inks on FSC®-Mix certified paper.

The authorized representative in the EU for product safety and compliance is Penguin Random House Ireland, Morrison Chambers, 32 Nassau Street, Dublin D02 YH68, Ireland, https://eu-contact.penguin.ie.

Create meaningful moments with gifts that inspire.

CONNECT WITH US
live-inspired.com | sayhello@compendiuminc.com

@compendiumliveinspired
#compendiumliveinspired